The Bethesda Preludes

The Bethesda Preludes

Walt-Christopher Stickney

THE PUSHKIN PRESS

Library of Congress Catalog Card No. 82-81058
ISBN 0-943046-00-9 HDBK
ISBN 0-943046-01-7

Some of these poems have appeared in **The New York Quarterly**, **Move Magazine** (London), and **The Washington Broadsides**.

The drawings are done with charcoal, pastel, watercolor, and prismacolor and are 9″ × 12″ and 11″ × 14″. They appear courtesy of Joel Krosnick, Alan Lomax, Arnold Wesker, Tony Abeson, Patti Chambers, and wCs.

Special thanks to William Claire, Charles Plymell, Susan Quasha, Barbara Raskin, Dr. Adolf D. Klarmann, Christopher Cornford, Brian McCollum, Sam Foxworthy, Stephen & Amy Jackendoff, and Patti Chambers.

The Pushkin Press has been funded by The National Endowment for the Arts and the Eugene & Agnes Meyer Foundation.

This book was designed and typeset by Open Studio in Rhinebeck, N.Y., a non-profit facility for writers, artists and independent literary publishers, supported in part by grants from the New York State Council on the Arts and the National Endowment for the Arts.

The book was printed by United Color in Cliffside, N.J.

Cover art, known as **Russian Soul on Strings**, is by wCs.

The Pushkin Press
1930 Columbia Road, N.W.
Washington, D.C. 20009

Printed in the U.S.A.

Contents

The Bethesda Preludes

for my father

Variations

1

...the night. n the life-lighter comes by
wid his heart. wid touches! wid considerations!
n the townspeople begin 2 shine-back
at the stars.

2

...at which excessive borders? standing!
in front of which doors do u want yer poet
2 come? from steps of some unseen temple
the self-fed dog stumbling on 2 n 3
paws, blind, out-of-love.

3

...my daughter's coronation...n the dressing
of her hair. a thousand brushes from the
baltic-mermaid on the waves. little stars
over her breasts...so the peasants aspire
2 be burned.

...daughter...even az they invite n u dance,
continue 2 b kneeling wid the crown

once my song.

prelude no. 1

Some time after the benches r frozen, empty,
we will confer wid ourselves, sparing no rejoinder,
pursuing no relief, no shortened phrase;
inside ourselves az we're inside r rooms
the easy banter of remembered little thoughts
going nowheres will go somewheres
n explode.

why, the year round, every year?
we've sat in twos toward any multiple,
confused by many lips, whose lips?
passing by r phases, ourselves, particularly r issue:
that lines n shadows shape, spread, on r faces;
that we seem slower
n 2 willing 2 seekout the benches everywhere.
it can't last beyond the next snow.
n so the 1st step, step n forget
that a sound iz due from the walk beneath, walkers beside u,
that familiar sights permit a lazy peace n contentment.
they once would but won't no more.
it's not az if we r all abandoning, severed, quit,
but rather we begin something az natural az before,
only from now there'll b more me,
more u.

look at the crowded space by a crowded distance!
u've but a war fought from below ground.
the lights flash. iz light helpful?
the cries come. when iz a whistle-burst ever a sign?
how much does anything, a world, contain?
n what iz overflow? empty? in your life?
so! around an early morning fountain
a child skippers his boat,
iz voyaging on the only uncrowded sea.
alone? when yesterday 5 sailed
thru the beginning of september?
he don't kno it at all.
he always counts his crew.

i kno u r not children now,
tho u may still speak of em.
there ain't those chances 2 play so endlessly,
4 seasons r az one 2 em in their 1 fleet season
n all places possible in only their miracle,
but u n i, i've tried by myself,
r divisible, can divide.
(the words been 2 long buried.)

i'd b silent n let u b az u've been,
but i've sat next 2 u talking worlds n lives,
az tho they were remote,
simply places n happenings n also
no one's relinquished the chat.
mainly we all saw 1 another. or did we even?
iz that how it? Loneliness? i kno it iz.
it iz n many other things attach themselves.
n these sweetly reveal your greatest fear:
"Lasting" in the more swift ascendant night,
the nights coming out of the ground,
in your days, n accelerating day.

summertime ain't hushed but easy n high,
so we watched flowers n their bloom,
the children 4 their sport,
listened 4 birds jus back whistling,
n retired in this every summer scene
carrying the very little unending accord
into the winter intact.

but now that the snows n freezing have begun,
perhaps they'll b remarked. i ask u "take a good look."
n like the white earth,
change 2 yer clearest self, adjust,
n press yer mind's fingers deep into the plain
n unveil that stretch of drifting winter.
having discovered being there later u'll move.
if but 1 of u disappears in that greater stillness,
fails 2 spring after feeling its urgent mystery,
i'll probably kno it n protect it.
together by ourselves we'll all
kno that 1 of u wuz wid us 2 b gone
n then lead on 2 "what about that 1 of us?".

u r my friends.
i can only call u that
having been beside u n not having branched.
yet if i went thru the parks
n cried "disassemble" rather than "remark"
would u even listen?
who amongst u would turn towards his own circle?
n who would feel its path?

i don't like 2 think it, but have i been deceived?
so many shy flowers come out before the snows melt,
below the mountain in the unprepared: dc meadow.
have i confused the month, the season of u?
r u dead so soon, always blasted, or still?
u've stood the cold?
u maintained yer color or chose a new 1?
u achieved some small elegance, abundant all of u?
so many flowers?
that iz no outcome! no!
having heard many things, all things in a crescendo,
u ain't inspired silence n yer thoughts nor moved.
no freezing but 4 myself.
i divine a new chaos in the midst of which
i close my eyes n substitute the sky.
precisely! i dance........on tears.

a reverence for life

prelude no. 2

and O......pray 4 us someone!
we've grown without ever having prayed.

n don't leave me here all alone.
i don't kno anything about it.

u went right by az i went deeper.

my room in the city remained small az my soul.
on white nights i lit it or took it 4 walks
or drank it desperately.
tho somehow u'd b quicker
n think while i wasn't listening.

some love sincerely never reaches us.

so soft candles n old horses sleep brilliantly on their feet.
n millions of little people travel together on their knees.
n there r punk angels sitting in trees perfecting the fall.
n r rude winters will always b close n warm.

yet my passions give way 2 pity.
i deliver n receive without a changing of voice.
u must hear the hunger n misery n loneliness.
alot of the sobbing iz yours.
the heart says human life should b
but there iz suffering.
i will ease it.
i can't.
n we suffer.

i'd only climb n never stop

or like a piano   develop after arriving
at 1 place   4 some time   more ways   up n down

or simply put the ocean on backwards n break.

we foresee 2 well.
enuf iz enuf.

it's not that it's been going on 4 so long.
(the bar iz still open. the church iz still open.
the fields r unusually open.)
but it's 2 cold 2 sit in any of em.
i lie here in u.

sex iz dragging like industry n the united nations.
no competition jus monopoly.
n i don't kno anything about it.
so it's yer move.

the price of sanity iz a life without ecstasy.

how rich 2 b poor?
how polluted iz r mirror?
how beautiful your happiness iz.
they ain't ever considered such unassisted flying.

i'd create a yellow cadillac wid power steering n powerbrakes.

inquire after me . . . i've taken a shower in the capitol.

we contend individually wid storm.
my idiots, my others, my self.

i walked away from 1 father n still relate.
u never quit yer specialty.

all humanness iz achieved now n a sacrifice 2 mankind.

it ain't what we b but what we do.
we'll bleed wid roses till r names have reasons.
we'll obey the strength of the spirit.
we require this willingness 2 suffer.

if the clear night fails
2 release its stars

then.
if.

it iz devastating.
it iz gentle.

we, who had prided ourselves on r fragility,
have known a curious faith.
it iz in everything.

the evening comes 2 me n pennsylvania.

i must always swear in peace.

prelude no. 3

not a damn thing more frightening than life

when we outa short dreams
n put on the wind wid bare shoulders, a bent neck,
a face towards an inner theme that's irresistibly heaven
but tinted by some desert, the fever of a modern sea.

we move towards the sky wid r hearts.
r bodies r evolving n wildly here.
we reclaim miracle from each obstacle wid r sleepe.
there r many in what we can expect 2 b in the daye.
beyond these r only the smoking endless canals
of man's soule, the night, the vibrating unimagined,
n a few rare mad notes in gold hand softly opening
2 some blissful century of intelligent fire,
of quiet loves,
of tireless movement,
or just some rainy morning
that won't stop calling us 2 work.

n all of this iz in the aire.
n 1 dancer leads u down az a river.
n there r others like him.
without costume. without directions. without.

a god? he iz 1 of em.
within the history of every universe.
n if u ask, we exist without him.

i want n don't want 2 need him having seen him,
1 force behind a force offering me 2 my co-natures.

it's all right 2 smile in town.
u've stepped forward wid your shoes.
we still have many hats 2 tip.
az 4 truth . . . dying on crossed wires, so light, so cheap

n how many gods maintain a field:
its soil n sun, being root n worm,
rock n water, all the green plants n red animals.

n how many r reeling in my city?

n when will u find them all, in what time,
n recognize how different u've become because of em?

u carry a pantheon!

such excess!
n we try r luck on holidays?

o dancers lift us before r eyes
n let us watch n follow.

let us join your hands.

we've changed movements in the wings.
we've stayed together wid shifting partners.
we've eaten under the table beneath leaping houses.
we've been swept away wid the leaves.
we've extended r arms n kisses n farewells.
we've been carried into the night wid r daughter.

n who taught who how 2 dance?

rather what iz it 2 dance without effort?

come up then or don't learn of memories,
of simple streams,
the harp, the violet, n secrecy.

                    i'd gladly clasp the robe of some
indeterminate saint, 1 who wuz frozen in the throes
of "do" n making his quiet way 2 many sad places
that have been specifically mapped az places 2
lose oneself. wearing an old ladies' dress,
ripped from some latterday boutique full of metal
n hair, leather n cloth on which designs of
lightning n thunder were inventories of famous
names (like jean d'arc, michelangelo, francis
of assisi, etc.), he'd intoxicate religion
wid humor n delay, 4 me, the conclusions that
had seemed foregone n almost acceptable.
recall that a desperate saint, a madcap saint
recently twisted his motorbike in the sea
or on the desert. he wuz unsure where 1 washed
or where 1 drowned being an accumulation of
alternatives himself. he iz worthy of r
reverence n r tendernesses. i kno nothing
of the origin of tears. i cried 4 that man
without disturbing him. i smoke down by
the pond. i dance there when everything else
haz been exhausted. so begin somewhere...n
later we'll skip over each other az an
ending.

if we have 2 live by lacing unfeeling arms,
it seems we do,
then somewhere on this earth,
tho i wuz at interposition n trying 2 care,
sadness will forever.
4 all the softer words,
for all the companionship of nights n days,
4 repeated covenants,
for love of the detested,
4 love of the blind,
for continents of flowers,
still we r not masters of seasons n ourselves.
n yet, how strange!
this union of islands iz innocent
n we barely notice:
the horizon iz gone.
did we kno it wuz there?
conscience of dreams!
we've wanted inaccessable toys n had em,
mirrors of mirrors,
mirrors of the world moving,
ship wrecks, wrecking sea,
thunder in the trigger of the clouds,
all accidents without injury,
all toys from where we've sat.
imagine how that spins
n this jumps,
this flies,
n this . . . . this goes off 2 itself.
o leave me alone while i love u.
i m still a boy amazed.

prelude no. 4

there iz yer frosted breath.
there iz a valley of snow.
there iz a field of children eating glass
az birds hang from embracing trees n bleed like flutes.
n u will go n u'll pack yer mind wid socks.
4 we live thru winters at these poles.
n it should b cold. so it's barren. we crave extremes.
n what makes us small, u often disappear,
endears me 2 the stars az so many of us r poor.

i lie into my sleep az others flee into a lavish night.

i'm tired of arts that point away.
i find little trace of love or care.
a commonhood of grasses iz waving under us.
i've just escaped from every jail n every hatred.
i can't reserve good judgment.
i welcome the alliance of rains into my hair.
we might become popular wid jus r hands.
i'd surrender europe 2 africa instantly
n undergo antiquity n steaming forest in a variety of soups.
russia serves potatoes az we adore senseless things.
that simplicity. this powerless friend of true kings.
n death.

n what r u doing wid your life?
n what r u saying wid your languages?

u have dispossessed the universe.
n we praise confusion n the infinite sources of details.
these numberless odds n oddities r commentary on r attention.

i stare at myself after going 2 u n blush.

so blind jogging pilgrims on minor roads 2 glory n madness...

i been on the subway ever since.

the foremost souls r writing books!

yet their evasive drama weaves thru time
like hot religious soldiers
n ravages the schools n confiscates the white houses:
n no thing changes.

the underground line never stops tho we get off somewheres.

n even tho more wonder lies in their exclamation points
than in r tears n in r deaths

journeying iz not the same az praying.

they do not see this cuz they don't read.

if this iz a time 4 confession,
they hear n it'll do u good,
all peacemen 2 yer untried feet
n tamper wid the world n the gods.

i believe in neighborhoods.

we have the right 2 love n save 1 another.

children r we young enuf?

Tomorrow is the duel

prelude no. 5

say of me...i wuz an interpreter of wars,

innocent of italic histories,
apprentice 2 no subtle knight,
aide-de-camp wid no muttering general,
 1st chef on no submarine,
navigator of no terrible jet,
secretary on no strategic council,
saluting no militant commanders,

merely 1 of thousands in the pit wid dying men,
distressed by ribbons, holding letters
n photographs n bandages up...

4 killing leaves me everywhere dead.

there iz no time 4 endless war.

(we r in step 2 meet 1 another in better ways.)
these studious troops, this electronic famine,
the young n nervous coveting some star invasion over lunch,
that wild drugged patriotic defense that rocked the jungle silly,
them heroes who delivered the moon b spilling badgas onto holyland,
n those professeurs of recent torture who visit
life's convalescent n healthiest,
(n folks that's most of us)

i don't kno what 2 say 2 em.

we r yer sisters fathers brothers.
yer mother won't even come downstairs.
she's sick of raw meat.

"so antie tell yer uncle.
friend tell yer friend.
sister tell yer brother.
cousin tell yer cousin.
we're goin 2 the country.
momma, don't u wanna go?"

so prepare the playgrounds 4 handshaking!
then jus go at it like exercise.
there r no atomic games today.
weird smiles spread round n kids grow n outgrow.
n u see what it means 2 stay out of it all.
i'd almost forgotten it.
n u r a veteran of foreign backyards?
did u stab any underwear or lead an epidemic?

there r no slight weapons on sale tomorrow.
there r only numbers on sale yesterday.
even a photo can't describe the reality.
who can afford another person's death?

we decorate instead of correcting ourselves.
2 many symbols of which freedom in ancient n failing eyes.

if u were 2 go hunting wid me 4 them?

if we were 2 visit each other wid ourselves?

each warrior iz a genius on a leash.
each battalion iz a nursery in the mud.
each army faces nothing unless it faces itself n runs.
many of u have seemed like people n lived 2 die in peace.
thru these brown wet binoculars i describe an inferior vision.

the future of man haz 2 do wid greater love n greater service.

trumpets 2 sympathy n trust n patience!

those ragged cowards at their homes (in civil dress)
r my teachers n my children.
they wash their faces wid the morning.
they cleanse their hearts wid madrigals n trees n forgiveness.
they may b listening 2 the faroff n the nearathand
while they lift the smallest baby onto the largest horse n go in.
they endure the art of dying n the art of living.
they plea 4 black equal woman justice rights.
n they r the 1st 2 die
being 2 much ignored n 2 much in love.
n they stand where we stand when we're up 2 it.
n they gonna lie into a roomy grave
n conduct the ballade of the gutted race.

or i might open this righthanded tomb n petition nature
before we plague the heron in its tranquil marsh,
or frighten that butterfly asleep on the bell,
or shred the old calendar before the new year's conquered us.

why must i b right?

i'm sure we'll b cruelly processed n in-isle'd
among the dead dying

unless we create (wid emphasis)
a union of shelters 4 being

or (there r those of u who'll come late)
get curious past crying

n cry out: LIVE WID US

prelude no. 6

there iz in the cavern of the merest bell.
there iz in the echo of butter on bread.
there iz in the frailest youth a mother without.
there iz a lonely calculus erasing infinity.
there iz an oblivious scripture that says whatever twice.
there iz a pitiless orchestra that strings up old slaves.
there iz panic n whispers n an orange path thru the hills.

n we r luminous pistols hiding.
we've lost the agency of night.
n there iz no coverlet 4 the sea.
n there's no pure reason … baby, i said no.

so i purchase an alley between my ancestor's gloom.
n i curry yer dogs wid narcotics n films.
we r poor typists in a convicted office.
the undertow of the street iz phosphorous n revolution.
n we'll fish wid r hearts 4 worms i guess.

az it iz
i hear u nothing sometimes operator im thru.

there's no returning 2 where we should've been.
this sheet iz pale n irreducible.

the laundry stinks inside the model's perfection.
n we r handed epic murders, rotting scaffolds, n disease.
we peel thru stained glitter in the newstand's church.

n even now . . . alot of us r missing.
tho i m right here.
n u were drafted early.
n volunteers r on the phones raising the count.

settle nothing but what soars beyond decision.

coca cola haz put a rubberband round my continent.
while they r helping the wildflowers dribble,
we may az well study at the burlesque n vote 4 jesus.
the mariners r free when they pull out their ships.
we should agree on the classics n get on wid it.
here n there the very white land of seabeaches.
my messianic audience iz whistling like six-year olds n buccaneers.
my dancing invalids never touch ground or get reviewed.
my prisoners gnaw on sorcery n make alota sounds like beer.
n i'm persuaded by retarded eyes n deaf hands.
n i'm married 2 a library of wings n thighs.

this restaurant of lamps iz crowded wid moths.
there ain't enuf light in here 2 go on.

read by listening n rejection in the dark.
sort a word 2 letters n epiphanies of letters or don't.
carry yer basket into the flowerbeds of lips.
siphon the liquid spirits of speech into bone.
the most real confluence iz a shovel or else.
taut muscle, feinting, wet cheeks sea'd: or plant a tree.
we forever read like glass that murmurs hysteria.
n we wayfare outside seasons n beyond the ken.

still, there iz a transparent government
where we meet r lovers n caress.

let me do the honors

prelude no. 7

n then once i softly . . .

on my way from the perimeters of man
n tired reverie n flanneled belief

2 tutored visions of joy n sorrow
upon a boy outside his home n shaking.

he moved beside me az i passed
like an exiled self

n reached 4 my hands
the very moment i remembered his.

we can neither die nor b born twice
but we can

n like 2 trees we went out of the forest
wid r roots n r branches

1 topless birch, 1 sprouting pine,
n into each other 4 a comparison of souls

n the delights of lonely mind.
thru no doorways or pathways

we felt helplessly like chance
n so came 2 pacing n sharing 1 another.

few children learn 2 b themselves
n 2 chamber such madness of silence

while the tag ends of their growing-up r swallowed:
o like birds n like fish n like the stillest stars.

he deepened my little
n i only touched his hand.

n so like infant magi leaving man 4 sleep or night
we descended 2 the miniature of things

n we sealed r gifts n like perfume we went out
n touched r age full of grieving n daymares n lies.

iz there anything he didn't have or wouldn't find?

hadn't i danced wid him before we met?

many layers unfold 2 new peoples n old ways
n then obscure again trancelike into stone.

mate in youth! boy in terror!

i wanted 2 notice u
n resurfaced the past

2 its origin of sliding moments,
character of irresponsible dreams.

we've seen angels wedded 2 dictators
n priests fully behind the cannon.

n i dare not reweave such potent abracadabra
az the tapestries r jewelled wid sperm n pus.

n don't b worried by the now of things.
we can tear the frontpage out of the radio.

i believe in

n u'll wear my shirt n carry my gloves.
n i m yer father n wife.

n we r flooded wid food-n-rent.
n we believe in everydays n stills of scenes.

so hold on 2 a dog.
my brothers will instruct u 2 yer restful self.

az it iz yer vision iz flawless n sleeping wid bugs.

u young ones at questioning
r never quite questioning

like elders when they ask n frown.
no diary of a cathedral will advise u 2 fly.

so i led u into skies n in n out of clouds
n started sympathies in yer eyes n heart

2 summon what shredded paradise hides
from yer mind like an awakening treasure of pain.

so i made a son of u,
more brother of u

than i ever did 2 my opaque family life.
we r thru wid the wilderness.

we've made out a check 2 the holy.
my compass iz freaking in prayer.

will u ever want a home again?
boy, i'll never kno u more!

no clipped tongues. no cut-throats.
i won't see u betrayed out here.

i learned from u
how 2 tremble in ignorance,

how 2 fear myself before knowing,
of shoelace problems,

the trial of forks n spoons,
we began wid knives!

of bony n sensitive angles,
we must have taught 1 another!

n where my rights have varied, gone,
n why i now alone.

we r 2 precious 2 b together.
we detract from what difference each of us iz.

we've noted routes thru all the elements.

n we arrive at "just me" n "jus u."
we r in the wake of all subtleties.

we r bending
2 the single instance of each life

written above a tune.

2 many of r companions never feel the sun
n gravely settle down the sea-road

at the bottom of which finds their faces
tragic, imploring, n their eyes no clearer,

not seeing further but simply deep,
so deep they look at simple "goodbye."

do i need 2 say it?

i have no remedy 4 death.
i've no poison 4 life.

i ain't fixed myself in a spot.
i use sidewalks n benches 2 n from the world.

i supply myself wid meanings 4 my returns n my relatings.
inspiring fresh beginnings!

we always must renew such boyhood n inquire
az it happens just az it iz.

prelude no. 8

i've been out here bout 10 days

or iz it years?
n where'd my good manners go?

n can i have planted my hat

or my boots in the key
2 that simultaneous chop suey joint

where columbia road revises saturday night
n we went off on a lofty drunk

n printed fresh food stamps on the spanish walls
in morbid letters wid fierce color?

we r eating r migrant souls away!
jus tomatoes! wid black beans! on watermelons! over rice!

this iz serious business.
nearby the hopeful people would open at 9

n close authentically when the paper curtain
came down bout 5...5:30.

n r dialogue wuz crucified in the park.

n like every exasperating tragedy
no actors r left 2 play pool.

n we arise in 3 days n try again, amigos.

n rollcall in my misty bar
iz by maiden names n full of announcements

n decorated by sex n established by incident
n recorded by fishermen n flooded wid guilt

n accompanied by horns n completely a joke.

n the next minute they'll tell u 1 thing
n then "jus take a nap,

the sun goes down 2 tomorrow"
or something else may happen.

it don't make no difference

whether millionaires r sucking on their bloodfields
whether emiliano iz sitting on his roof wid a llama
whether the pawnshops r lining guitars wid opium
whether the women r mobilizing their homes wid rape

n whether it do or it don't it will
cuz everybody's caught wid their pants down.

n congress iz in a jazz session jus up the hill.
n the supreme sport iz milking in a steam bath.

n we r on a loose flight over r humanity.
it never occurs 2 u 2 yawn or substitute a fullback.

this america takes pleasure in its future.
n don't the world look in pain on tv.

the past iz such a strange friend
wid a beautiful face n real long legs.

n r imprecise dance iz so ultimately sad n unforgettable.

i pursue happiness at that tip furthest from u
n lead u 2 it like a drink beside some bread:

yes, we r starving   apart.

my last feeling iz that all love needs a choice.

zzzzzzzzzzzzzzzzzzzzzzzzzzzzzzzzzzzzzzzzzz

father hear me out!

the 9th

...broadside opera...my perilous labor on the morning bus.

i may become perfectly extinct before lunch
2 attend in velvet bones the premiere in the streets.

only now in the local flop house, near the bakery, in my
side-streets of paris, on the florist's backporch, where
josalie does her toilet n i brew a perfumed myth, or in
barcelona where the canaries r in a perpetual jig, beserk,
or sweden, my own white trough, where 1 or 2 princes
wet their pants n their nurses help em out
n interpret me:

there u have nonsense! the opera!

the prescription iz non-stop whatever-u-like.
u have a trembling nostril, something bluer like a cold?
here's a rag! wrap yerself in it!

i believe there must b a trumpet erect somewheres,
scattering hot baroque from 9 to 5. i believe

a soprano iz on the lily pad about 2 take a dive.

believe me, during this nervous, holy work,
every brilliant librarian will b asleep.

the parliament of the crickets haz jus quit the heath.
their cause will b 2
                    sanatize my venice!
ah, swamp of arcady, i swam under yer bridges
n gave myself 2 the smells n sighs.
i fished up tintoretto.
i recycled the young scarlatti.
but did it matter?
the erotic scenery wuz returned 2 the children.

but now . . . the Overture of the Lampposts.
ready? "PIGEONS!" let the snow go!
listen, "plop," 2 the birds.
it's easy 2 B when u listen 2 the birds.
the morning's music, the rooster's stuff: old cereal, wine,
n stale jam tarts. n there's jus 2 parts,
n one's yours n the other's mine.
so let's harmonize wid the alphabet,
get animals in on the act.

u can go anywhere wid a voice.
n this 1 goes round the world!
u can drink vermouth till u fly.
pushkin said so n did.

look, abelard's in the suffragette's chorus!
so whatdya want?
susan b. anthony?
mister, come-on, can ya pipe on that pencil or not?
or jus blow me a dime.
i can't warm this corner n waste my time.

the welfare aria's committing screaming cavity in this bough.

i kno, so the snail gives a slimy check. but how
else might i buy my daily mirror? Sweet Horror!

i've got 2 bury this spectacle in the cemetery by sunset.

... broadside opera ... my perilous labor on the evening bus.

WALT-CHRISTOPHER STICKNEY was born August 30, 1944 in
New Orleans, D.C., Md., Pa.,N.Y., England, France, Sweden, Italy,
and W.Va. He received a B.A. in English and Comparative Literature
from the University of Pennsylvania. His books include **To Night:
Little David on Mouth-Harp, Cover My Souls,** and **one n five
minute pose-pomes.** He has performed widely in Europe and the
United States. He received the first individual grant award from the
D.C. Commission on the Arts and Humanities in 1977 (for Literature).
He has given three one-man shows of his drawings and has
participated in numerous group shows. He founded The Pushkin
Press in 1974, edited **Piano, a flowing journal,** and is the director of
44 Covers for the Locked-up n Locked-out, a traveling exhibition of
visual art by 44 Washington artists that becomes an environment in
which music, theatre, dance, and poetry performances and
workshops are given in hospitals, prisons, and schools. He lives in the
Adams Morgan community of Washington, D.C.